Gray Zone

WHEN LIFE SUPPORT
NO LONGER SUPPORTS LIFE

Deborah Day Laxson

Copyright @ 2013 Deborah Day Laxson.

ISBN 13: 978-1-59298-980-5

Library of Congress Catalog Number: 2013909118

Printed in the United States of America

Second Printing: 2015

17 16 15   5 4 3 2

Cover and interior design by Laura Drew.

Beaver's Pond Press
7108 Ohms Lane
Edina, MN 55439–2129
952-829-8818

To order, visit www.itascabooks.com
or call 1-800-901-3480. Reseller discounts available.

For Bill

AUTHOR'S NOTE

Most books are best if read cover to cover. But I've tried to write this book so each chapter could stand on its own if you didn't have the time or desire to read cover to cover. As a result, some information may be repeated from one chapter to the next. I've also written in short sentences and paragraphs, hoping to have a conversation with you. I've taken liberty from time to time to use conversational grammar such as *they* when perhaps *he* or *she* would have been proper English. When you're in the Gray Zone, you can barely think, let alone read.

ACKNOWLEDGEMENTS

This book could not be written without the support of family and friends.

I especially want to thank Kelli Spencer, for opening my eyes and reminding me of my gift and life purpose; Reverend William and Linda Meier, for extending kindness and compassion to a total stranger in time of need; Karen Zimmer, for being my friend, for nudging, nagging, and otherwise providing positive encouragement to continue when I would have stopped; and Maryjude Hoeffel, for your red pen, your gifts of wisdom and calmness, and for sharing your story with me and being a kindred soul.

Thank you to my wonderful family: Tina, Bill, Donald, Alan, Beth, and Christopher. You are the best of both of us. Beth, thank you for standing next to me and reminding me of what I already knew in my heart of hearts.

Thank you, Dr. Girum Lemma of Coborn

Cancer Clinic, for your daily visits while Bill was in the intensive care unit. Your caring and compassion eased my fears.

I also thank Dr. Scott Davis and the staff in the intensive care unit at St. Cloud Hospital for their sensitivity and compassion at a time when I was terrified of making the wrong decision. Actually, I was afraid of making any decision. Dr. Davis and his team consulted with me many times, trying to provide as much information as possible so I could understand to the best of my ability Bill's prognosis day after day. I can't thank you enough for your extraordinary care of Bill and just as extraordinary care of me during those difficult days.

And finally, thank you to Kevin Spellacy, attorney at law, Quinlivan & Hughes, P.A., for helping Bill and I write our wills and health care directives, and in the process, introducing me to the concept that sometimes modern medicine may prolong death instead of supporting life. Kevin, thank you. I took your wisdom with me into the Gray Zone.

Preface

Bill was my husband and best friend for close to thirty-five years.

Although we were getting older, we were still young enough to have plans, to have dreams, and to have a bucket list to complete.

We suffered aches and pains attributed to what doctors frequently called the "at your age" or "as we age" syndrome, depending on the age of the doctor.

Life turned on a dime with Bill's diagnosis of multiple myeloma, a form of terminal cancer.

The treatments were harsh, the side effects

permanent, and Bill's physical decline apparent.

Although Bill stayed relatively positive emotionally, the quality of his life physically was poor.

Bill told me a month before he died that he was ready to go. He had written all he wanted to write in his journal and said all he wanted to say.

He was ready.

I wasn't.

However, because he was ready, I knew intuitively his time was near.

I always assumed I would be there when he died.

I never thought I would be the one starting life support to keep him here.

Nor did I think I would be the one to remove life support and let him go.

I wasn't ready.

I never would be.

What Is Life Support?

In simple terms, life support begins when a medical team uses equipment, such as a ventilator, or takes measures, such as intravenous feeding, to provide artificial support for essential bodily functions and keep the patient alive.

We are blessed today with all the advances modern medicine affords us.

At the same time, we are cursed with all the advances modern medicine affords us.

Life support can be both a blessing and a curse.

Sometimes life support starts without you even realizing it.

BILL'S STORY

Bill was diagnosed with multiple myeloma, a form of terminal cancer, on October 28, 2008, in the emergency room of our local hospital.

It's amazing how many details of the day stick in my mind.

It was close to noon.

Bill was sixty-five at the time and had rarely been sick during our thirty-two years of marriage.

The day started roughly for Bill. He hadn't been able to get out of bed in the morning due to excruciating pain in his back. He couldn't breathe deeply enough to even call out to me.

I was at the other end of the house and didn't know he was in trouble.

It took him almost forty-five minutes to get out of bed

and find me.

In typical Bill fashion, it took me another two hours to convince him to go to the emergency room.

We didn't talk much on the drive to the hospital.

He thought he pulled his back. I thought maybe he had a kidney infection.

We were both wrong.

Test after test came back telling us what it wasn't.

Finally an x-ray showed lytic lesions on his bones, which suggested multiple myeloma. A bone marrow test would later confirm the diagnosis.

We went from "normal" to "terminal" in four hours. Life was never the same.

You will find that I use the word we *when talking about Bill's cancer.*

What affected Bill, affected me, too.

So, we had cancer.

We suddenly found ourselves learning the difference between a diagnosis and a prognosis.

Bill underwent tests too numerous and painful to share.

He started chemo treatments, dealt with side effects, and started taking drugs.

So, so many drugs.

Our heads were spinning, and our life spun out of control.

We learned to redefine normal and move forward through what limited treatment options Bill had available.

We got our affairs in order.

We updated our wills.

We created our first health care directive.

We agreed to act as each other's health care agent and make medical decisions on each other's behalf.

I don't think we understood what that meant.

I know I didn't.

Bill underwent an autologous stem cell transplant in 2009.

Bill sailed through the stem cell transplant and returned home within six weeks.

He stabilized and held steady through 2010. He didn't get better. But he didn't get worse, either.

We both came to terms with his cancer.

He took the time to plan his funeral and his burial.

We had the tough talks. Bill was very clear about what "quality of life" meant to him and what he expected from me as his health care agent.

I listened carefully. I supported the decisions he made about his current life, and I understood what he expected of me.

Intellectually, I understood this was about Bill and his wishes. I understood he expected—no, needed—me to follow his directives.

But I learned there is a world of difference between intellectually understanding something and emotionally experiencing something.

We talked about what we might both expect as the cancer progressed.

I was silently hoping Bill would not get worse and live a long, long time.

He was hoping to die before he became an invalid,

a burden to loved ones and society, with someone spoon-feeding him and wiping his chin and other places.

Bill began to have trouble sleeping, as he had read somewhere that he would most likely die in his sleep. He worried he would die in our bed and I would wake up to find he had passed during the night.

And as we processed all of this, the days quietly, stealthily slipped by.

On Friday, February 11, 2011, Bill developed a fever. We made the now routine visit to the emergency room.

He was treated, the fever came down, and we went home just as we'd done all the other times.

On Saturday, February 12, Bill blacked out while I was running errands.

We went back to the emergency room on the advice

of the on-call oncologist.

This time, Bill was admitted to the hospital for observation.

Later in the day, he was moved to a higher-priority section on the hospital floor for close monitoring.

It was touch and go for all of Saturday and Sunday with his fever steadily climbing.

By 5:00 am Monday morning, Valentine's Day, Bill's fever broke. We were through the worst—or so we thought.

We expected him to be in the hospital for another couple days and then back home.

We were wrong.

While Bill had been doing great in the early morning, his breathing became labored during the early afternoon. It got progressively worse by the hour.

I was literally watching Bill turn gray as the oxygen levels in his blood dropped.

Finally, he was barely able to breathe and as a result could barely talk.

The staff asked and I confirmed that I was Bill's health care agent and that the necessary paperwork was on file at the hospital.

As Bill continued to get worse and the minutes ticked by, the staff talked to me about options.

One option was to put Bill on a ventilator to get the oxygen levels back up.

By 9:00 pm, he was in intensive care, hooked up to a ventilator.

What I didn't realize at the time was that Bill had pneumonia and was now on life support.

What Is the Gray Zone?

Life support starts out innocently enough.

The steps leading up to life support start with a trauma or a significant decline in one's health that results in the need to provide medical assistance to the body.

Life support "buys time" for the body to recover on its own or for the medical team to provide additional treatments in the hope of returning the body's ability to function on its own.

In the case of pneumonia, the lungs begin to fill with fluid and lose the ability to provide the body with the life-sustaining oxygen it needs.

If the lung function declines to a point where the oxygen level gets low enough to be life threatening, the patient is placed on a ventilator.

Using the ventilator provides oxygen and supports the lung function while the body tries to recover and return to normal.

Life support is begun exactly for that purpose. To support one's life.

Let's stop and think for a moment. Think about the continuum of life and death.

Picture it as a line with life at one end and death at the opposite end.

The Gray Zone is that fuzzy area in the middle when life support measures subtly change from supporting life to prolonging death.

LIFE   THE GRAY ZONE   DEATH

The Gray Zone is that spot on the continuum where the intent of supporting life slowly evolves into grayness and where it is not clear if the treatments and life support measures are helping or not.

Are the life support measures in place really supporting one's life, or are they now prolonging one's death?

DEB'S STORY

The way to the Gray Zone started like any day, with a now routine trip to the emergency room.

Bill was running a fever.

He'd had them before. He got infections more easily now because his immune system was so compromised from the stem cell transplant and all the cancer-fighting drugs.

Having a fever was nothing new.

We'd go to the emergency room, get diagnosed, get additional fluids, get more medicine, and be home before the end of the day.

We'd done it before.

We'd do it again.

We went into the emergency room on Friday, February 11.

Bill got diagnosed, got the additional fluids, got the new medicines, and we went home.

It was as we expected.

Been there.

Done that.

No worries.

On Saturday, February 12, Bill blacked out while he was home alone.

He had been feeling fine when I left. And other than feeling slightly lightheaded when I returned, he seemed fine.

Still, the blacking out was different, so we called the on-call oncologist.

We were advised to make the trip back to the emergency room.

This was new.

We didn't usually do back-to-back emergency room visits.

This was also the first time the emergency room nurse asked Bill if he had a DNR (Do Not Resuscitate) order in place and asked if he wanted to be brought back in the event his heart stopped.

He said, "Sure, bring me back. I've got eye surgery on Monday." He turned his attention back to his smartphone and continued texting family members.

Nobody asked anything about a DNI (Do Not Intubate), so ventilators and artificial breathing never popped up on my radar.

This time, Bill was admitted to the hospital for observation.

We'd done this before, too, so we assumed we'd be home in a day or so.

Been here.

Done this, too.

Still no worries.

Over the next twenty-four hours, Bill's fever got worse. He was moved to another section on the floor, where the nurse-to-patient ratio was lower and he would get more focused care.

His fever continued to climb for another twenty-four hours and then finally broke in the early morning hours on Monday, Valentine's Day.

By 5:00 am, Bill's temperature returned to normal.

We were confident we'd be going home soon.

During the doctor's rounds early on Valentine's Day, Bill was told he could probably go home by Thursday.

We were relieved.

We were going home later in the week.

Things would be okay.

We were wrong.

By early afternoon, Bill wasn't able to breathe normally.

The nursing staff ordered oxygen therapy. That helped for a while but didn't work for long.

The oxygen treatments kept getting more and more intense, but he still wasn't able to breathe normally.

Bill was showing early signs of respiratory failure.

He was in pain, gasping, and turning gray.

I would have done anything at that point to stop his pain and ease his breathing.

Because Bill could barely breathe and was unable to talk, the medical staff looked to me for permission to move Bill to the intensive care unit and put him on the ventilator.

My instinct was to keep Bill alive.

I gave permission to sedate Bill, intubate him, and hook him up to the respirator. This would allow his lungs time to rest—and to heal, as I thought at the time.

I gave that permission without hesitation or reservation.

It never occurred to me that we had just started life support.

The first step toward the Gray Zone began with that decision.

While I knew he was being hooked up to a ventilator, I really didn't even think about that being life support.

And when Bill was sedated, I didn't think of him as

being in a medically induced coma.

I didn't think at all.

I went along with the flow and kept focusing on what it would take to bring him back.

I simply wanted to do the right thing so Bill would get better.

By now, Bill had been diagnosed with pneumonia and septic shock.

It seemed the ventilator was helping Bill. His skin lost that gray color, and all the monitors indicated Bill was holding his own.

He was kept sedated for a day or so while his body fought the fever and his lungs tried to heal.

The staff periodically gave Bill a "sedation vacation," meaning they stopped the sedation and allowed Bill to "surface," or regain consciousness.

During the first sedation vacation, Bill knew where he was and was able to wiggle his fingers and toes when asked.

He was in pain, though, because when sedation is started, pain medicine is withheld.

At this stage of multiple myeloma, there is a lot of bone pain.

We started the pain medicines, but when Bill began gagging on the tubes in his throat, he was immediately sedated again.

And while he seemed to be holding his own, more and more intervention was needed to keep Bill stable.

Bill was hooked up to the ventilator and being fed through tubes.

Then he needed dialysis to help his kidneys filter his blood.

And then he needed insulin shots.

And then...

As the days blurred by, very quietly, very subtly, very slowly, we entered the Gray Zone, where it was no longer clear or certain that all the life support measures in place were still supporting Bill's life.

In the Gray Zone

The Gray Zone is a difficult place to be.

It's that fuzzy place where it's not clear if the life support measures are really supporting life and allowing the body to heal, or masking the reality that death is inevitable.

If you are listed as the health care agent and the patient is unable to speak for themselves, the medical staff looks to you for guidance.

The staff gives you options and possible treatments, and then they look expectantly at you to make a decision on behalf of the person you are representing.

Bluntly stated, that's basically an "oh, crap" moment for you.

While you may have innocently agreed to be listed on someone's health care directive, you probably never really thought about what that meant, and you most likely assumed you would never have to fulfill your duties.

You may have replied with, "Sure, sure, whatever. You're my friend [or loved one]. Of course I will."

But because you never gave it a thought, you now find yourself panicked that the medical staff is now looking to you to make decisions about what treatment your friend or loved one will receive.

They're looking to you for direction, and you're looking back at them, wishing they'd tell you exactly what to do.

They can't, and they won't.

They'll give you options, probabilities, side effects, outcomes, five-year survival rates, and all sorts of medical terminology and jargon that doesn't mean anything to you.

You want assurances.

You want guarantees.

You want your friend or loved one back.

You want this over and everyone all better.

And the medical staff is still looking to you for guidance and permission, and you're still looking at them, feeling afraid, angry, and helpless.

All you really want are clear, concise answers; a clear direction; and someone to tell you exactly what to do next.

And that's exactly what you don't, and can't, get.

Instead, you have more questions than answers and suddenly more opinions that confuse things instead of clarifying things.

What life support measures do you allow?

If your friend or loved one does survive, will their quality of life be acceptable to them?

How do you make decisions on their behalf?

Most of us do not have medical degrees, yet we still have to make decisions in the midst of very detailed medical jargon we don't understand.

How can you get the right information so the decision is clear?

How do you make sense of conflicting medical information?

How do you address your fears, the fears of your family, the fears of your friends?

How do you account for the person's will to live?

How strongly do they want to live?

Can they overcome and recover from the physical challenges they are dealing with at this time?

How can one person with a 5 percent survival rate make it back from the Gray Zone and live, and yet another person doing seemingly well suddenly take a turn for the worse and die?

When do you hold steady and continue the treatments and life support measures?

When do you let go and stop?

When is enough, enough?

You make decisions based on what you know from your medical team and what you know about your loved one's definition of quality of life.

You do the best you can.

You're in the Gray Zone.

It's a really lonely place to be.

DEB'S STORY

The machines, the medical routines, the drugs, all helped Bill's body keep functioning. But at some point, it was no longer clear to me that they were supporting his life.

As the days slipped by, I began to wonder if instead they were prolonging his death.

I worked closely with the doctors and the nurses, and I searched online for information regarding treatments, medicines, options—in search of anything that might give me hope.

Bill was still hooked to the ventilator to help him breathe.

He was still being fed intravenously.

He now needed dialysis, as his kidneys were no longer filtering his blood effectively.

He then needed insulin shots.

More and more intervention was required to keep Bill alive.

I stood at the foot of his bed and looked at all the IVs, heard the beeping of the IVs when they needed attention, heard the whisper of the ventilator, and heard the nurses' voices when they spoke to Bill as though he were awake.

I saw the change in the staff members' eyes and heard the change in words spoken to me as the hours and days slipped by.

I could feel Bill slipping away, too.

The doctors now talked in terms of weeks and

months to recover and that he would most likely re-quire permanent assistance if he did.

He would leave the hospital with significantly less physical capacity than when we checked in on February 12.

How long ago that seemed now.

While there was a quiet determination in all of us to help Bill fight, there was now the slow realization there was little to fight for.

He had terminal cancer.

The pneumonia didn't change that.

If Bill made it back now, it still meant he would die from cancer, most likely within the year.

At this point, I realized with certainty that all the medical interventions were no longer supporting Bill's life but clearly prolonging his death.

I had promised Bill long ago I wouldn't let him die alone.

It would have been easier had he died in his sleep.

I thought he'd die on his own accord, on his own terms, when he was good and ready.

I never thought I would be the one making the decision to let him go.

Beyond the Gray Zone

We are all born to die.

It's just a matter of when and how.

For some of us, our friends or loved ones may ask us to be their health care agents and make medical decisions on their behalf.

I repeat, on *their* behalf.

Our friends or loved ones asked us to set aside our opinions, our beliefs, and our fears, and act instead as though we were them.

In order to do that, we need to understand how

they define "quality of life."

What's important to them?

What are they willing to fight for?

Or, stated differently, what are they willing to live with?

It's not what we think they should fight for or live with.

It's not about us.

It's about them and what they want.

They've entrusted us to make those decisions if and when needed.

Most of us agree to take on the role of health care agents assuming we will never have to actually exercise that responsibility and actually make decisions about medical treatments.

Many of us are right—we will never have to make those decisions.

Some of us are wrong.

Some of us will have to make the decisions we agreed to make but really never, ever thought we'd actually have to make.

None of us making those decisions ever have enough information.

All of us are terrified.

Few of us are ever ready for the Gray Zone and all the decisions made there.

Even fewer of us are ever ready for *the Decision*.

DEB'S STORY

It is really hard to give up hope.

To admit that death is always inevitable.

I think it's instinctive to delay our own death as long as possible.

Certainly, if we are asked to make medical decisions on behalf of our friends or loved ones, we want to give them as much time as possible to recover and return to the state where they can make their own decisions.

When it's our friends or loved ones, even if they're really sick, we still want them healthy and back to our best memory of them.

We pray for a miracle and pray we won't be asked to make the Decision.

I sat and held Bill's hand for days and watched the machines and staff work to keep him alive.

I held his hand as an anchor to this physical world and to remind him I was still here and wasn't ready to let him go.

It felt right that first time he came up from the sedation. I could look in his eyes and see his life force there.

He was there, and he'd make it back.

The next time the sedation was removed, he didn't open his eyes, he didn't respond, and I couldn't tell if his life force was there or not.

But Bill's hand was still warm.

His heart was still beating.

The ventilator still whispered as it kept breathing for him.

And the staff still worked hard to keep Bill's body alive.

As the days continued to pass and as I still held his

hand, it became slowly clear that more and more medical intervention was required to keep his body alive.

If I were truly honest with myself, I realized at some point we were beyond the Gray Zone.

All the life support in the room was no longer supporting his life but merely prolonging his death.

I stood at the foot of the bed and looked upon his now-frail body.

This strong, vital man, this hero to his kids, would not be happy with what he saw.

Nor would he be happy with the quality of his life if he managed to come back.

In my heart of hearts, I knew I had to let him go.

For the first time in days, I left the ICU to clear my head.

I ended up at the local mall, buying Bill a new suit. One he'd wear forever.

I cried, then cried, and cried some more.

I went back to the ICU and spent one more night holding his hand, praying for a miracle that would bring him back to the way I wanted him.

The answer came quietly when nothing changed that night.

The machines still beeped, the ventilators still whispered, and nothing changed.

The Decision was made.

I needed to honor his request of me, to preserve his quality of life.

Which meant I had to let him die.

In the morning, the IVs and the machines were removed.

The only sound in one small room in the ICU was the sound of Bill breathing on his own.

I didn't know what to expect once the machines were removed, but I think I knew in my heart of hearts that he wouldn't wake up and I'd never get to look into his eyes and tell him goodbye.

Instead I held his hand through the day, stroked his face, and told him I would miss him and I would be okay.

I lied and said what I thought he needed to hear.

I gave him permission to go.

I was terrified.

My heart was breaking as I continued to hold his hand throughout the day as his breathing became more and more labored and his heart rate slowly dropped.

And finally stopped.

Epilogue

There are no words that can adequately describe the pain and the emptiness I felt leaving the hospital the night Bill died.

My worst fears had been realized.

My nightmare was complete.

I was now a widow.

To this day, I don't remember anything after pulling the car up to the hospital door and loading up all the things that managed to creep into Bill's ICU room over our ten-day stay.

I'm not sure how I drove home.

I walked into my house, collapsed on the stairs, and cried.

No, I didn't cry. That would be too tame.

I was physically and emotionally exhausted.

I sobbed, I wailed, I grieved.

I finally made it from the stairs and headed into our bedroom—no, wait—*my* bedroom now.

And I looked straight into Bill's eyes.

The life-size portrait taken for our thirty-fourth wedding anniversary hung over the nightstand and was the first thing I saw when I walked into the room.

Bill had looked straight into the camera lens when the portrait was taken, resulting in the sensation of looking straight into Bill's eyes regardless of where you stood while looking at the portrait.

Standing in front of the portrait, gazing into Bill's eyes, my world righted again, and the pain I felt eased.

That life-size portrait saved me.

It gave Bill back to me and took away the sights of a frail man in an ICU attached to machines and IVs. It replaced those images with the sight of the man I knew and loved.

I left the Gray Zone behind and walked straight into the Fog Zone, called grieving.

Appendix

SO YOU'VE BEEN ASKED TO BE A HEALTH CARE AGENT

It starts out innocently enough.

Your friend or loved one needs someone to make medical decisions on their behalf if and when they are unable to make those decisions themselves.

They need a health care agent.

They need someone they can trust, someone they know will be in charge and make medical decisions when they can't.

Generally, the conversation is a simple one, sounding something like, "Hey, I need someone on my health care directive. Will you do it for me?"

You say, "Sure."

And that's generally the end of the discussion.

Your name goes on the dotted line, and your friend or loved one files the paperwork. You all go back to living your lives without a second thought.

What you may not have thought about is what you just committed to doing.

Your friend or loved one may have a medical event someday that renders them unable to make medical decisions.

While you may have *intellectually* understood that you agreed to make medical decisions for them, do you *emotionally* understand what you agreed to do?

You just agreed to set *your* opinions aside and make the decisions *they* would make, based on *their* definition of quality of life.

You agreed that in the chaos of a medical event, you will step in and give direction on what medical treatments they will receive or, more importantly, what treatments will not be started or what treatments will be stopped.

It will already be a difficult time for you if it gets to the point where your friend or loved one is unable to make their own medical decisions.

There may be a chaotic medical event if there's an accident, and decisions will need to be made quickly, with little or no time for discussion or research.

The medical event may be a slow decline as

a terminal illness takes its toll and their health slowly declines.

Or the medical event may be surgery. You are on standby while your friend or loved one is under sedation and a medical decision needs to be made.

Every situation will be different.

Regardless if the medical event evolves quickly or slowly, the result is the same.

Your friend or loved one needs you to step in on *their* behalf.

Will you be ready?

Do you really know what *their* wishes are?

Do you know *their* definition of quality of life?

Did you talk to *them*, and more importantly, did you *listen* to their answers?

And did you ask yourself if you have the *mental fortitude* and *emotional maturity* to step outside of your fear, your wishes, to make the decisions *they* would make if they could?

Be honest with yourself.

Can you respect and act on *their* wishes?

Can you make the decisions you know your friend or loved one wants you to make, even though you may be going against the wishes of their family and/or friends?

Can you consciously allow your friend or loved one to die a natural death by either not allowing life support measures to start or by removing life support measures once it's believed those measures no longer support a quality of life your friend or loved one wants?

If the answer at this point is no, you owe it to yourself and your friend or loved one to respectfully tell them no and explain why.

If, on the other hand, the answer is yes, have you thought about what might happen?

Every situation will be different.

Every outcome will also be different.

You will never have enough information to make a decision with a guaranteed outcome.

You won't get a "do over."

You may have to make decisions when you are tired, scared, and out of hope.

You will have to fight your rational mind and not make the decisions you want to make if they are not the decisions you know your friend or loved one would have made.

You will have to set your fears, your wishes, your hopes aside and remember what you agreed to do, which was to make the decisions your friend or loved one would have made if they were able to make their own medical decisions.

If you're lucky, when you agreed to become a health care agent, your friend or loved one gave you documentation that defined "quality of life" for them.

If you have that documentation, you can reread it and refresh your mind about what they would want.

But you still won't have all the information you want or need.

Chances are, the health care directive doesn't cover the exact scenario you will be faced with. So you'll be left doing the best you can and honoring the intent your friend or loved one had in mind when they defined their quality of life.

You will still be looking at the medical staff to give you direction, as they're the ones with the medical degrees and must have all the answers.

But the medical staff can't give you guarantees

and they can't make your decisions for you.

The medical staff will be waiting for you to give permission to start or stop medical treatments as the health care agent for your friend or loved one.

Everyone will be looking at you to make the decisions that in your heart of hearts probably terrifies you.

I am a health care agent for my daughter.

I now know what I may be faced with in the future.

And yet, I have to remember that I represent a different person of a different age, who will have a different medical event and who has a different definition of "quality of life."

I will still have to make *her* decisions.

If and when I have to do this again, here are some things I'd consider:

How old is she now?

> *There's a difference if someone is twenty-nine and healthy versus eighty-eight and frail.*

Are there any underlying health conditions?

> *Things are different if someone is in perfect*

health before the medical event versus if some-one has a preexisting health condition or some form of cancer.

And there's a difference between cancers (e.g., breast cancer or prostate cancer that can be "cut and cured" versus terminal cancer that can potentially be "controlled" but not cured).

In the case of terminal cancer, what is the current life expectancy of your friend or loved one?

Based on the medical event and the recommended treatments, what is the predicted quality of life and would that be acceptable to her?

Here's how one person described an acceptable quality of life: "As long as I am independent. I can live with physical adjustments such as artificial limbs, catheters, a wheelchair, etc. as long as I can take care of myself. What is not acceptable to me is if I have to rely on someone/society to take care of me. I would be miserable and would pretty much make everyone taking care of me miserable too. I would not be a gracious patient. Don't make me live like that. Please."

DEB'S STORY

By this point, I may not have left you with much hope.

Please don't be discouraged.

What you are reading is influenced by my own experience in the Gray Zone.

My story did not have a happy ending.

Since then, however, I've talked to other people whose friends or loved ones were on life support with very low probabilities of surviving yet came back from the Gray Zone just fine.

Remember, every person, every situation, and every outcome will be different.

Keep hope until you can't.

I wish for you and yours the best possible outcome that meets the highest good for all concerned.

Look for these titles by
Deborah Day Laxson:

The
Fog Zone

SURVIVING AND FINDING
LIFE BEYOND GRIEF

Deborah Day Laxson

The
Joy Zone

GIVING YOURSELF PERMISSION
TO LOVE AND LAUGH AGAIN

Deborah Day Laxson